The Hannah Anointing

What People Are Saying About The Hannah Anointing

He makes the barren woman to be a joyful mother.
—Psalm 113:9

The Hannah Anointing by *Apostle Connie Strickland* is so beautifully written! Being a woman who has experienced what seems like an unending barren season, I could not put it down! It is a powerful story of love, pain, suffering, prayer, and perseverance; throughout the anointed pages of this book we see the sovereignty of God on display. So much Glory is released that we are still reading and building our faith on it to this day!

Only an Almighty, loving God could bring about such beauty in the life of Hannah. Thank you, Apostle Strickland, for telling this beautiful story of the Faithfulness of God. I am confident that through this book, many will be encouraged to stay the course to receive the revealed Glory of God. *Apostle Connie Strickland* is an excellent writer and teacher of the Word. Blessings and honor to you woman of God!

Minister Sandi Cook
Fountain of Life Global Ministries
Houston, Texas

Apostle Connie Strickland is an anointed prophetic vessel of the Lord in the areas of teaching, training, and proclaiming the Word of God. She is dynamic in deliverance and prophecy as she blesses Kingdom congregants throughout the United States and abroad. Apostle Strickland is an awesome gifted writer of several books that peer into the heart and command transformation!

The Hannah Anointing will bless you! It will encourage you to be persistent in your quest to birth what you demand! You will reach your goal by not giving in to your challenges as you strive to make your requests known unto God and get miraculous results! You will not be able to put this book down and will show immense growth as you digest these anointed chapters!

Prophetess Shelia Joy Josey Pittman
The Rock International Church
Houston, Texas

The Hannah Anointing

Birthing the Promises of God

Connie Strickland

Foreword by Dr. Patricia Ashley

The Hannah Anointing

Unless otherwise indicated, scripture quotations are taken from, **THE KING JAMES VERSION** (also called "The Authorized Version") of the Bible.

ISBN - 978-0-578-68305-8

The Hannah Anointing
Birthing the Promises of God

Published By: Destiny Publishing Group
3033 Bardin Rd. #1201
Grand Prairie, Texas 75052
Email; destinypublishinggroup@gmail.com

Dedication

This book is dedicated to my mother, Icerine Hunter who transitioned to be with the Lord on August 24, 2017. Her life was an epitome of the Hannah's Anointing. Mother not only presented her specific request to the Lord, but she loved interceding for others. I am a recipient of her answered prayer. I continue my mother's Legacy of Prayer and Intercession as I empower intercessors all over the world. Thank you, mother, for planting that seed! **A fulfillment of the word** in 1 Corinthians 3:6-7: *I have planted, Apollos watered; but God gave the increase. So then neither is he that planted anything, neither he that watered; but God that giveth the increase.*

Acknowledgments

I would like to thank God, Yeshua and Holy Spirit for inspiring me to write this book and giving me revelation and insight into Hannah's story. By His Spirit I was empowered to articulate what God is saying to YOU through this book.

I thank God for my children and grandchildren for pushing me and giving me words of encouragement that empowered me to overcome procrastination. Thank you, Marcus, Tiffany, and Erica, for always being supportive of the creative ideas that God is birthing through me. Thank you, Destiny, Alyssa, and Jazyiah (grandchildren) for always giving Nanna that hug when needed.

A special thank you to my spiritual parents Apostle David *"Windfall"* Pittman & Prophetess Shelia Joy *"Favor"* Pittman for their prayers and words of encouragement that they render daily. Thank you for teaching me the word of truth and compelling me to be all that God has called me to be. Your labor of love for me and my family, ministry, and businesses are highly appreciated

I thank God for Aunt Betty & Uncle Melvin McAllister, and Aunt Shirley & Willie Adkins who are two of the 3 sisters left of my mother's sibling that I can call and talk to and laugh about the memories of mother and the good times that our family share. Thank you, Aunt Betty, and Aunt Shirley, for your prayers

I thank God for AHOP (Apostolic House of Prayer) and all the prayer leaders all over the world that cover me and my family, ministry, and businesses in prayer. A special thank you to my spiritual daughter Trina Bradford and her prayer team in California that cover me in prayer.

I thank all my family and friends who continue to pray for me and LOVE me unconditionally.

And to my Readers, may you be blessed beyond measure. This book was birthed for YOU at this TIME!

Contents

Foreword

I've had the privilege of being in full-time ministry for over 35 years; it has been a blessing to use the Word of God, the power of prayer, and a love for people to see lives changed and women healed and set free.

I had the pleasure of meeting *Connie Strickland* at church over 30 years ago. I have had the opportunity to spend time with her to know her as a woman who loves God and people and wants to see them walking freely in their Kingdom authority. She is known to many in the Kingdom as an effective intercessor and powerful teacher of the Word.

The timing of the release of this book is perfect. We are living in a season of social distancing; grief, as well as the loss of lives, opportunities, and jobs are all the result of the global pandemic.

Many people like Hannah are experiencing barrenness as the result of unfulfilled goals, dreams, and expectations. We may be forced into obscurity, but this time of lockdown has released an opportunity to spend quality time in prayer. This book will encourage you while igniting your passion to release prayers that produce results.

Connie Strickland reminds us that like Hannah, we can cry out to God, trust in the promises of His Word, and know that his plan is to take you from an empty place to the amazing land of prosperity. God wants to bless you so that He can use your life to draw others to Himself.

In this book, you will be encouraged by the life of Hannah; you will learn how God is able to answer your prayers and turn your barren situation around. You will be reminded of how God is not limited by your circumstances. He can act despite your disappointments, unfulfilled dreams, and the situations beyond your control. This is a book that you will enjoy and desire to share with friends and family. You will want to keep it within reaching distance so that you can read it again when you need the encouragement to press forward in prayer.

Dr. Patricia Ashley
Conference Speaker/Teacher
Author of "Marriage is a Blessing"
Dallas, Texas 2020

Introduction

Each of us has experienced "seasons" in our lives where we face uncertainties, question our desires and motives, and wonder if God is truly with us. In these seasons, we eventually realize that our purpose is to fulfill the plans that God has chosen for our lives. The Bible reminds us of this in Ecclesiastes 3:3: "To everything there is a season, and a time to every purpose under the heaven."

This book depicts the life of a godly woman, Hannah, who endured a season of barrenness; yet, she continued to trust God. In her barrenness, Hannah suffered pain and torment from her adversary, Peninnah. Hannah was unaware, however, that everything she endured would eventually result in her ability to fulfill the promises of God.

We are never sure of *why* we endure life's difficulties until we arrive at the other side of the struggle. We all will go through trials, tribulations, and tests, these are just *seasons;* they are not indicative of the future. God's word encourages us not to focus on those things that we see with our natural eyes because they are *temporary.* We must focus on things that are *eternal.* (2 Corinthians 4:18). Change is inevitable; but, the promises of God are eternal!

Maybe you can attest to the season that Hannah endured because you once were there, or you are there now. Maybe you are enduring a season where you feel unproductive and obscure. God's word declares that He will never leave us nor forsake us. Sometimes, however, it feels as if He is not there. Hannah certainly felt as if she was cursed because every woman in her community had children. Hannah was barren because the Lord had closed her womb.

Please embrace this truth! Whatever trial, test, or suffering that you must endure in life is purposeful. In other words, *God always has a purpose for allowing you to endure suffering.* His purpose and plans will manifest according to Jeremiah 29:11, which reads: "For I know the thoughts that I think toward you, saith the Lord, thoughts of peace, and not of evil, to give you an expected end."

We will learn from Hannah how she presented a specific request to God that changed her life. Hannah kept the faith! She did not give up! God had to alter Hannah's perceptions and perspective so that He could reveal to her a wonderful blessing — she would birth more than just a son! Hannah would birth Samuel, a great prophet, priest, and judge. God used Samuel to bless and restore an entire nation. Likewise, God wants to use you to bless others.

I PROPHESY that as you read, you will observe God's plan unfolding for Hannah and His plan unfolding for you! Each chapter provides an assessment to challenge you in your observation, interpretation, and application for personal growth. You will gain clarity and insight for your current season to BIRTH out the PROMISES of God!

Chapter 1

Hannah's Barren Season

The book of 1 Samuel Chapter 1 conveys an interesting story of a man named Elkanah. Elkanah had two wives—one was named Hannah; the other was Peninnah. Because Hannah's name is mentioned first in scripture, we believe that she was Elkanah's first wife. But, why did Elkanah have two wives?

The wife whom Elkanah loved, Hannah, was barren because the Lord had closed her womb as we read in 1 Samuel 1:5. The word barren in Webster's Dictionary means to be unproductive or unfruitful. Elkanah could not handle the shame of being alienated or ostracized because his first wife was barren. He resided in a society where families were embraced and revered. "Desperate for a child, Elkanah found a wife who could give him one."

Polygamy was never God's original intent; however, Elkanah lived at a time in which polygamy was permitted. This form of marriage was not acceptable to everyone. Polygamy is only mentioned a few times in the Old Testament. I do not know of too many women who would want to share their husbands with other women, do you? Whenever two women are in the same house, sharing the same man, you can certainly expect jealousy, competition, and negative attitudes.

And, remember when Sarah in her old age was barren and she wanted to give Abraham a son? Sarah suggested to Abraham that he have sexual relations with her handmaiden, Hagar, so that he could have an heir. Abraham agreed to the offer; thus, Hagar had a child whose name was Ishmael, meaning "God will hear." Yet, that is not the end of the story nor was it the end of the consequences that Abraham and Sarah would face as a result of not waiting on God.

If you read Genesis Chapter 16 you will gain more insight. Sarah was not cognizant that this offer she made to her husband would open a "spiritual door" that would bring shame to her family. Abraham declared to Sarah that Hagar's son would not receive the inheritance because it was promised to Jacob, a true heir. (Genesis 28:13)

I can attest to Hannah's frustration about being "unproductive" because the female womb was created to produce! Hannah probably suffered from low self-esteem and rejection from the other women in her community. Women like to gossip, and you can imagine that she was the talk of the town. But if they only knew what God was planning to birth through Hannah's suffering!

We learn in Romans 8:18 that "the sufferings of this present time are not worthy to be compared with the glory which shall be revealed in us." God was preparing to manifest something greater in Hannah's life. He would do more than just bless her with a male child; her prayer all along had been quite specific. We will learn more insight regarding specific prayers in *Chapter 3, The Power of a "Specific" Request.*

Expect Your Season of Barrenness

Every believer will encounter a season of barrenness. You may be in that season right now. Do not become weary SEASONS will change! Do not let other people—even family members—

Every believer will encounter a season of barrenness.
You may be in that season now.

define you based on your current season. God has a perfect timing for everything. He does not move in time as we know it, the "Chronos;" rather, He moves in the "Kairos." Only in God's *appointed time* will His promises manifest for you. In the meantime, you will persevere and endure through the process just as Hannah.

I feel the power of God moving upon me to pray for you. May I pray for you right now? Holy Spirit is going to pray through me as this prayer is released for YOU!

"Father, in the name of Jesus, I want to thank you for the reader and pray that your will be done in her life according to Jeremiah 29:11, which reads: "For I know the thoughts that I think toward you, saith the Lord, thoughts of peace, and not of evil, to give you an expected end."

I pray that if she is in her barren season that you give her the strength to persevere and that your praises will continually be in her mouth.

I pray that you will give her a revelation of what you are speaking to her in the midst of her situation. Give her clarity, Oh Lord and remind her of your promises which are Yes, and Amen!

I prophesy that she will see with Your eyes and that the Holy Spirit will be the loudest voice she hears! I decree that every plan of the enemy, external and internal, be eradicated now in the Name of Jesus!

Let her not become weary in well doing, for she shall reap if she does not faint, according to Your holy word.

I pray that you will give her a mind to study your word and the word will be planted in her heart. Help her to confess Your word daily so that she can change the atmosphere!

Thank you for manifesting your promises in her life!

In Jesus' name I pray! Amen."

Remember Beloved, the same God who closed the womb *will open it at His appointed time!* Stay encouraged and persevere!

God's Purpose for Hannah's Barrenness

Let us observe a familiar scripture many believers declare when they need insight regarding their current circumstance. Romans 8: 28 reads: "And we know that all things work together for good to them that love God, to them who are the called according to his purpose."

God has a purpose for every situation we face. We may not understand it immediately, but in time we will.

Hannah was about to receive the revelation of God's plan for her season of barrenness. God used Hannah to birth the greatest prophet of that era. He used her seed to restore Israel back to Him! (At this time in history, the Bible tells us that the Isarelites had alienated from God and began to worship the gods of their enemies).

In the midst of any challenge, I always ask God what He's teaching me? If we do not learn in our challenges, we will find ourselves revisiting the same or similar situation again. And, oftentimes, these situations are passed from generation to generation. We must remember that every trial, test, circumstance, or challenge we encounter is to make us better, and, to make us more like Jesus.

As you delve through each chapter, you will see how God changed Hannah's perspective. We know she desperately wanted a son and that's all she focused on. She fell into a state of depression and had to simultaneously endure harassment from Peninnah. Every day, Peninnah tormented Hannah, but, Hannah did not retaliate because she did not want to dishonor her husband.

One advantage that believers have (that our Old Testament friend, Hannah, did not have) is the power of redemption! Because we have been redeemed by the precious blood of Jesus, shed at the cross, we have received power and authority to apply to our circumstances. Hannah remained silent in the midst of shame and harassment. Silence is a powerful weapon when we learn how to use it.

This truth is revealed in Exodus 14:13: "And Moses said unto the people, Fear ye not, stand still, and see the salvation of the LORD, which he will shew to you today: for the Egyptians whom ye have seen today, ye shall see them again no more forever. The LORD shall fight for you, and ye shall hold your peace."

This is the word of the Lord as He spoke through Moses to the Israelites. The Egyptians held them in bondage for 400 years. God made a promise to Abraham that He would send a deliverer. He told them that He would fight for them and to "hold your peace," which is interpreted, "be silent." God will fight for you and silence your enemy simultaneously. Just as God told Israel to stand still and see the salvation of the Lord, He is speaking the same to you today!

God is Our Deliverer

I am so glad that I know that God is faithful! What about You? Can you attest to this truth? Have you experienced God's faithfulness in your life?

Hannah had an affliction that she suffered for many years. An affliction is something that causes pain, suffering, and torment. Hannah experienced all these emotions! I hear people complain of mediocre things such as a toothache, a job loss, or the fact that their husbands failed to put down the toilet seat; but, have they really suffered through an affliction as Hannah did?

There was an appointed time for God to deliver Hannah and manifest His promise to her. As we read herein, we learned that Hannah was in a polygamous marriage of which she had no control. She had to contend with her adversary, Peninnah, who took advantage of every opportunity to make her life a living hell.

> *Whatever your affliction is, do not allow it to consume you. God permits afflictions to manifest so that He can reveal His Glory!*

Just as Hannah, we too have an adversary according to 1 Peter 5:8: "Be sober, be vigilant; because your adversary the devil walks about like a roaring lion, seeking whom he may devour." We overcome our adversary by living the word of God daily. Living the word is the evidence that we have been transformed!

The affliction of being barren left Hannah in a hopeless state. As you continue to read each chapter, God will reveal to you that He was with Hannah in the midst of her affliction. Let's focus on a familiar scripture that most believers have memorized; it will be one that you decree during your affliction—Psalm 34:19: "Many are the afflictions of the righteous: but the Lord delivered him out of them all."

Now, this is good news. I live by this beautiful promise. You must believe that your barrenness is only temporary. Deliverance will come to you! Every promise that God has spoken to you will come to pass. Whatever your affliction is, do not allow it to consume you. God permits afflictions to manifest so that He can reveal His Glory!

No matter who you are in Christ you are not above afflictions! Sometimes your affliction may be more intense than others' afflictions, but do not measure the grace of God by someone else's affliction. God's grace is amazing! Embrace His grace to help you endure your times of affliction.

I once preached a message titled "The Blessing of Afflictions." When God gave me this message, I wrestled with it. How can there be a blessing in one's affliction?

No matter the degree of our affliction, we must continue to persevere, trusting God to deliver His best outcome. We must adhere to the admonition that we are to give thanks to God in all things. (1 Thessalonians 5:18)

Now, what's the blessing? The blessing is that God gets an opportunity to reveal His Glory through your affliction. When you come out you have a testimony. When you share your testimony, people will be blessed. So, hold on, Beloved! God will deliver!

Chapter 1: Hannah's Barren Season
Application for My Life

1. What is the definition of the word "barrenness"?

2. What was God's purpose for Hannah's barrenness?

3. Who was Hannah's adversary? What role did this adversary play in Hannah's season of barrenness?

4. Who or what is your adversary? Why is it important to recognize your adversary during your barrenness?

5. Do you believe that everyone will endure a "barren season"? Why or why not?

6. Why does God allow us to be afflicted? What reasons can you list?

7. What scripture gives us the assurance that God will deliver us from affliction?

Answers to Life Application Questions

1.

2.

3.

4.

5.

6.

7.

Chapter 2

Perseverance: The Key to Your Breakthrough

In this chapter we will observe the power of perseverance. Despite Hannah's hardships, she remained faithful unto the Lord! She did not give up! I am grateful that history records her story of perseverance, aren't you? The word of God says that if you faint in the day of adversity your strength is small (Proverbs 24:10).

Webster's definition of perseverance is "continued effort to do or achieve something despite difficulties, failure, or opposition; stead-fastness." Do not allow difficult situations to overtake you. Keep moving; your change will come!

Many people today are giving up and giving in. Depression is real and frequently leads to suicide. As we read Hannah's story, we ascertained that she was depressed, but she did not allow her depression to subdue her. She continued moving despite her circumstances. We can learn much from Hannah's perseverance.

Let's examine Hannah's life and observe some circumstances that she endured. We see that Hannah:

➢ Resided in a household with a jealous woman who tormented her every day

➢ Endured mockery from Peninnah as the family travelled annually to Shiloh

➢ Endured the insensitivity of her own husband

Do you know why Peninnah was jealous of Hannah? She was the wife with children; however, she did not get the attention she desired from her husband. And, Peninnah was quite aware of Elkanah's love for Hannah. The more he expressed his love for Hannah, the more jealous Peninnah became.

The Bible says that Elkanah gave portions to Peninnah and her children but to Hannah he gave a double portion. 1 Samuel 1: 4-5 reveals this truth: "Whenever the day came for Elkanah to sacrifice, they would give portions of the meat to his wife Peninnah and to all her sons and daughters. But to Hannah he gave a double portion because he loved her, and the Lord had closed her womb." Elkanah believed the double portion would appease Hannah's depression.

It is one thing to have to wake up and face your enemy in your home and another when you are faced with perpetual torment on the way to your place of worship. History reveals that it was the family's tradition to travel to Shiloh—approximately twenty miles from Jerusalem—to make their annual sacrifice.

What was Elkanah thinking when he asked this question in 1 Samuel 1:8? "Then Elkanah her husband said to her, "Hannah, why do you weep? Why do you not eat? And why is your heart grieved? Am I not better to you than ten sons?"

This is certainly not a question you ask a barren woman. But what Elkanah tried to convey to Hannah was that *he loved her despite her barrenness.* He did not perceive the severity of her torment while residing in a home with a second wife who had children. In the midst of this arrangement, Hannah never brought confusion to the home. She did not allow her emotions to dishonor her husband. She remained faithful in prayer! May we learn from Hannah's persistency in prayer.

Hannah never brought confusion to the home.
She did not allow her emotions to dishonor her
husband and she remained faithful in prayer!

Persistent in Prayer

The word persistent is defined as "continuing firmly or obstinately in a course of action in spite of difficulty or opposition." We certainly see persistency in Hannah! She continued in prayer and in her devotion to God.

Prayer is a vital weapon in our lives if we choose to use it. We cannot endure the challenges of life without prayer. It is a command from Jesus; therefore, it is not an option. Jesus led by example because He was a man of prayer. He arose early and prayed for his disciples and the lost souls who would receive salvation through his disciples. In John Chapter 17, you will see that Jesus was fervent in interceding for us! In Luke 18:1-8 we will find the compelling story of the tenacious and persistent widow:

"Then Jesus told his disciples a parable to show them that they should always pray and not give up. He said: In a certain town there was a judge who neither feared God nor cared what people thought. And there was a widow in that town who kept coming to him with the plea, 'Grant me justice against my adversary.'

"For some time, he refused. But finally he said to himself, 'Even though I don't fear God or care what people think, yet because this widow keeps bothering me, I will see that she gets justice, so that she won't eventually come and attack me!'"

And the Lord said, "Listen to what the unjust judge says. And will not God bring about justice for his chosen ones, who cry out to him day and night? Will he keep putting them off? I tell you; he will see that they get justice, and quickly. However, when the Son of Man comes, will he find faith on the earth?" (NIV)

The widow was persistent in asking until what she requested manifested! This passage of scripture is controversial to some believers. They believe that when you present your request the first time that is it!

I am not debating here, but there is a lesson to learn from this parable. The word of God encourages us to pray without ceasing! In other words, do not stop praying!

> *In spite of her opposition, Hannah did not stop praying. Do not be deterred in any way from being persistent in prayer!*

Despite her opposition, Hannah did not stop praying. My prayer for you is no matter what you are going through today, you will not be deterred in any way from being persistent in prayer.

Breakthrough is Coming!

I want to encourage you to keep moving in the midst of your affliction! You may not identify with what you are going through as an affliction, but Hannah certainly did! Let's review 1 Samuel 1:11: "And she vowed a vow, and said, O LORD of hosts, if thou wilt indeed look on the affliction of thine handmaid, and remember me, and not forget thine handmaid, but wilt give unto thine handmaid a man child, then I will give him unto the LORD all the days of his life, and there shall no razor come upon his head."

In Hannah's case, she experienced emotional pain and suffering as a result of her barrenness. I encourage you to read 1 Samuel Chapter 1 for insight regarding how Hannah's prayer of supplication and travail manifested a breakthrough for her. We will discuss suffering in more detail in Chapter 5 and travail in Chapter 6.

My Christian journey began at age 29. Church mothers always encouraged me with this statement: "Hold on! Your *breakthrough is coming!*" Yes, I would hear this statement all the time, but no one ever conveyed to me what it really meant. What does it mean to "hold on"? It means that you must continue to believe what God has promised you no matter what. Breakthrough is when you see the manifestation of what God has promised! The word of God is true and everything that God has promised will manifest at its appointed time. You are closer to your breakthrough than you can imagine. Hold on! Change is coming!

The scripture reveals to us that breakthrough never comes without a battle. This truth is depicted in the life of King David. He identifies God as "the Lord of the Breakthrough" because God delivered David from the hands of his enemies.

This story is revealed in 2 Samuel 5:17-20: "But when the Philistines heard that they had anointed David king over Israel, all the Philistines came up to seek David; and David heard of it and went down to the hold. The Philistines also came and spread themselves in the valley of Rephaim. And David enquired of the Lord, saying, Shall I go up to the Philistines? wilt thou deliver them into mine hand? And the Lord said unto David, go up: for I will doubtless deliver the Philistines into thine hand. And David came to Baalperazim, and David smote them there, and said, The Lord hath broken forth upon mine enemies before me, as the breach of waters. Therefore, he called the name of that place Baalperazim."

David is being pursued by his enemies, the Philistines. Why were the Philistines trying to overthrow David and his army? They had heard of Samuel anointing David as king. They were outraged with jealousy. The Philistines traveled to the valley of Rephaim where they devised a plan to conquer David and his army. Smith's Bible Dictionary defines Rephaim as "giants." Rephaim also is translated as *"the valley of the giants,"* a spot which was the scene of some of David's most remarkable adventures. There, David twice encountered and defeated the Philistines. (2 Samuel 5:17-25; 23:13). David, being pursued by the Philistines, did not know what to do so he prayed. Have you ever been in this place? I am sure your answer is yes. The truth is, we all have been in this place. God gave David specific instructions and guidance he implemented. Divine intervention prevailed over David's enemies. David called the place *Baalperazim,* which means *The Lord of the Breakthrough!* Let's consider the five-fold ministry gifts as outlined in Ephesians 4:11-13: "And he gave some, apostles; and some, prophets; and some, evangelists; and some, pastors and teachers; For the perfecting of the saints, for the work of the ministry, for the edifying of the body of Christ: Till we all come in the unity of the faith, and of the knowledge of the Son of God, unto a perfect man, unto the measure of the stature of the fulness of Christ."

Do you see how these gifts applied to Hannah's son? And, what about the church (ecclesia) overall? The church would be in a better state than what we are in today if we were all unified in faith as this passage describes. Many believers are fighting one another. The devil, who is the real enemy, has deceived many in the Body of Christ to believe that we are *enemies of each other!*

You will not successfully eradicate your enemy if you do not identify your enemy. David knew his enemy! The Philistines were the enemies of Israel.

You will not successfully eradicate your enemy if you do not identify your enemy. David knew his enemy!

History reveals how God always destroyed the enemies of Israel. God loved Israel in spite of their perpetual disobedience to His laws. The Israelites, after all, were God's chosen people. Just as God loves Israel, God loves YOU! If you are in a battle today, know that God wants to fight for you. You do not have to fight this battle!

God spoke these words to King Jehoshaphat in 2 Chronicles 20:15: "The Lord responded through His prophet, Jahaziel. 'Listen, all Judah and the inhabitants of Jerusalem and King Jehoshaphat: thus, says the LORD to you, 'Do not fear or be dismayed because of this great multitude, for the battle is not yours but God's'."

God is saying the same to you today. You were created to win! Let go and let God! YOU must totally surrender everything to Him. Sometimes that can be difficult, however, He wants to lift your burden! The Lord of the Breakthrough is here. Let him fight for YOU!

Chapter 2: Perseverance: The Key to Your Breakthrough Application for My Life

1. What is the definition of perseverance?

2. Name a circumstance in Hannah's home that she endured?

3. Why was Peninnah jealous of Hannah?

4. Why did Hannah choose not to retaliate against Peninnah?

5. What must a believer implement in her daily life to live victoriously?

6. Why is prayer important to you?

7. What does the term "Baalperazim" mean? What scripture in the Old Testament reveals its definition?

Answers to Life Application Questions

1.

2.

3.

4.

5.

6.

7.

Chapter 3

The Power of a "Specific Request"

I am so glad that you made it to Chapter 3. What lessons have you learned from the first two chapters? Whatever lessons you have learned, I hope you will apply those truths to your life. In this chapter, we will observe the request that Hannah presented to the Lord. Every believer is familiar with Philippians 4:6, which reads: "Do not be anxious about anything, but in every situation, by prayer and petition, with thanksgiving, present your requests to God." (NIV)

The Greek word for requests means to petition or "beg". Those who know Him perceive that it is a privilege to express our requests to Him.

Most people tend to run to everyone but God in difficult times. We run to our spouse, our in-laws, the church mothers, and our pastor. Do you know that God is concerned about YOU? He delights in responding to your requests that align with His will.

Hannah's request was specific. She knew what she wanted. Let's identify if her request was motivated by a need or desire. Certainly, needs can be quite different from our desires!

For example, if you reside in Houston, Texas, possession of a vehicle is a need. You need a vehicle to travel to one region to the next. But, in New York possession of a vehicle is not a need according to statistics. Of all the people who commute to work in New York City, 39% use the subway, 23% drive alone, 11% take the bus, 9% walk to work, 7% travel by commuter rail, 4% he carpool, 1.6% use a taxi, 1.1% ride their bicycle to work, and 0.4% travel by ferry. What is the promise to a "need" request?

Let's observe Philippians 4: 19: "But my God shall supply all your need according to his riches and glory by Christ Jesus." We can all stand on this promise with confidence that God will meet our needs.

A desire, conversely, is wanting to have something, such as my personal desire to be married. I have never been married and my desire is to experience this God-ordained union before I depart from this earth.

I presented this "desire" request to God three decades ago and I am still awaiting its manifestation. My request is that God will send me a mate who would love Him more than he would love me. I cling to this promise and agree with Psalm 37:4, which admonishes, "Delight thyself also in the Lord, and He shall give you the desires of thine heart."

The word delight means "to please someone greatly." If your life pleases the Lord, He will grant you the desires (Hebrew meaning "requests") of your heart.

The word delight means "to please someone greatly."
If your life pleases the Lord,
He will grant you the desires of your heart.

Hannah's desire to have a son pushed her into a place of desperation. Have you ever been in this place? I have and it is not a comfortable place. If you feel desperate, you believe that your situation appears to be hopeless. In this scenario, you must continue to pursue hope! This was certainly the case with Hannah.

My point in sharing this truth and analogy is to show you that you must distinguish the difference between a need and a desire. What is your request to the Lord today? I encourage you to be specific!

Why a Son?

I conveyed to you earlier that Hannah knew what she wanted. Let's observe her request in 1 Samuel 1:11.

> "And she vowed a vow, and said, O Lord of hosts, if thou will indeed look on the affliction of thine handmaid, and remember me, and not forget thine handmaid, but will give unto thine handmaid a man child, then I will give him unto the Lord all the days of his life, and there shall no razor come upon his head."

Hannah prayed out of the anguish of her soul. This is called a prayer of "supplication." The Hebrew and Greek words most often translated supplication in the Bible mean literally "a request or petition." Therefore, a prayer of supplication is asking God for something to the point of pleading.

A prayer of supplication is asking God for something to the point of pleading.

Hannah was desperate for a son. Even though Hannah appeared to have devout faith, God had not blessed her with a child. She was certainly at the point of anguish, and she was pleading! Hannah was no different from the many women today who are believing God for a child.

Can you imagine taking a pregnancy test year after year and the results are always negative? I pray for all of you who are barren in this season that *God will open your womb! Not just your physical womb, but your spiritual womb!* I understand the frustration that results from the inability to conceive. Women get frustrated when they cannot conceive. For this very purpose (reproducing) God created the woman. God created Adam, then he formed Eve from Adam's rib, and, since that time, every human has come from the womb of a woman! We were created to reproduce mankind!

In Hannah's culture, it was honorable to have a male child. The son became the heir to the family inheritance. I challenge you to read 1 Samuel Chapter 1. You will see the hand of God on Hannah's situation even though Hannah felt as if God had forsaken her.

Many of us can attest that there are times in our lives when we are enduring the trials of life and it appears that God is silent. Just because God is silent does not mean that He is not working things out on our behalf.

I once traveled to a ministry assignment and as I looked out the window of the airplane at 36,000 feet, the plane appeared not to be moving! But the plane was certainly moving!

In that moment, God showed me this revelation: "When I am silent and it appears as if nothing is going on in your life, and you feel as if your prayers have not been answered, that is the time when I am moving swiftly!" God then said to me, "a SUDDENLY will manifest," which was quite powerful considering my current season. How can I describe this interesting word? A

"SUDDENLY" is an event that occurs when the favor of God is extended to you in an instant—the answer is manifested faster than a speeding bullet. In other words, people around you may still be waiting for God's answer while you have just received yours in an instant! This type of occurrence is a "SUDDENLY."

Our God is no respecter of persons. What He has done for me, He will do it for you (Romans 2:11). I decree a SUDDENLY for you! I have heard many testimonies of how God manifested a SUDDENLY in the lives of His people.

You see, beloved, just as God wanted to give Hannah more than a son, He wants to do something greater for you too! God revealed to Hannah His purpose for her son in 1 Samuel 3: 1-5: "Now the boy Samuel ministered to the Lord before Eli, and the word of the Lord was rare in those days; there were not many visions."

"And it came to pass at that time, while Eli was lying down in his place, and his eyes began to wax dim, that he could not see; and before the lamp of God went out in the tabernacle of the Lord where the ark of God was, and while Samuel was laying down, that the Lord called Samuel, and he answered, "Here I am!" So, he ran to Eli and said, 'Here I am!' for you called me."

In this passage we read that God is calling Samuel. God called Samuel three times; however, because Samuel was still a child, he did not recognize the voice of God. Just as many Christians today who have been in church for more than 20 years or so and can still be considered children because they do not know the voice of God. The point is that God had predestined Samuel's life before the foundation of the world. God chose him to be a prophet who would communicate His heart to the Israelites.

History reveals to us that the Israelites had alienated from the laws of God. Read Judges 2:10-12 to gain more insight. God always has a "remnant"! In the midst of this corrupt world where mankind has forsaken the laws of God, you and I are the remnant. Just as Samuel was the voice for his era, God has many voices that will speak to our current generation and the generations to come. I hope and pray that you will be one of those voices. This is my daily prayer: "Lord, use my voice to shake the nations and advance your kingdom!"

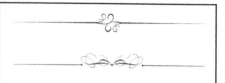

> *As we endure the difficult storms of life, we must remain faithful, because our faith will be tested. We must continue to stand on God's promises.*

God's Purpose Transcends Man's Plans

God was working according to His plan and He was not at a loss. We read in I Samuel 2:35: "I will raise up for myself a faithful priest, who will do according to what is in my heart and mind." When Hannah found herself in this hopeless situation, God was working out His plan. If Hannah's prayer for a son had been answered immediately, she may not have given him to the Lord. Her faith and her obedience to God was put to the test. And, God expects the same for us. As we endure the difficult storms of life, we must remain faithful, because our faith will be tested. We must continue to stand on God's promises.

No matter what circumstance you are facing, God has a purpose for it. I have often wondered what type of questions Hannah asked God regarding her barrenness. Maybe she asked the Lord, "What did I do?" "Why am I barren?" "Why does Peninnah gets to have sons and daughters and I don't?"

Sound familiar? We all are guilty of asking God questions. That is a good thing because the only way you will receive answers is to ask questions. Sometimes, however, you may not get the answers you want!

In Hannah's situation, God chose to *change her perspective* before answering her request. She did not understand at first that God had a purpose and plan for her womb. The Bible declares in Jeremiah 29:11: "For I know the thoughts that I think toward you, saith the LORD, thoughts of peace, and not of evil, to give you an expected end."

God was conveying to Hannah during her barrenness that He was still in control of the bigger picture. He had plans to bless Hannah not only with a son, but God also chose to bless a nation with a prophet, priest, and judge! God wanted to use Hannah's son to change the destiny of Israel! The Bible says that God can do more than we could ever expect or believe.

One of my favorite scriptures revealing this truth is Ephesians 3:20: "Now to Him who is able to do exceedingly abundantly above all that we ask or think, according to the power that works in us. To Him be glory in the church by Christ Jesus to all generations, fore and ever. Amen."

What are you believing God for on today? Have you presented a specific request before His throne? Whatever you ask of God is what He will hear! Please stay with me and Let's continue to the next chapter. God has more revelation and insight for us!

Chapter 3: The Power of a Specific Request
Application for My Life

1. What was Hannah's specific request?

2. What is the difference between a "need" and a "desire"?

3. What scripture can you apply to a need request?

4. What scripture can you apply to a desire request?

5. Why did Hannah desire a son?

6. Why did God close Hannah's womb initially?

7. Do you know God's purpose for what you are going through right now?

Answers to Life Application Questions

1.

2.

3.

4.

5.

6.

7.

Chapter 4

Suffering in Silence

A virtue that was evident in Hannah, which I greatly admire, was her ability to be silent in the midst of her suffering. Her pain and oppression were real, but she never said a word!

Even while she was being tormented and emotionally abused by Peninnah, Hannah remained silent.

Suffering is a part of life and no one is exempt from it. The rich suffer and so do the poor. All of God's people will eventually experience suffering during their life.

Suffering is a part of life and no one is exempt from it. The rich suffer and so do the poor.

Webster's Dictionary describes suffering as "conscious endurance of pain or distress." Let's observe the synonyms: distress; misery, and agony.

All these synonyms were evident in Hannah's life, but she embraced silence, a virtue that is absent in many of our lives.

Silence can be a powerful weapon if you learn how to utilize it. Many believers give place (opportunity) to the enemy because they talk too much. Ephesians 4:27 encourages us: "give no place to the devil." If you give the devil place, he certainly will take advantage of it. Oftentimes, when we are focused on our circumstance, we began to share things that we do not need to disclose. This disclosure is especially true for married couples.

Silence can be a powerful weapon if you learn how to utilize it.

Married couples must use wisdom when sharing their issues with others. So many divorces have occurred because a spouse shared something that he or she should not have shared outside the confines of marriage. I do not know why the Holy Spirit is leading me in this direction; maybe someone need to hear this!

Our society consists of many cultures that can attest to the reality of suffering. History reveals how numerous people groups have suffered as a culture. Statistics have concluded that Jews have suffered more than any other cultural group. The Holocaust massacre is evidence of this truth. The suffering that was imposed upon the Jewish people cannot be compared to the Glory that God has for them according to Romans 8:18, which reads: "For I reckon that the sufferings of this present time are not worthy to be compared with the glory which shall be revealed in us."

As we observe the Jews today, we can attest that God has restored them. Many Jewish people are returning to their homeland and they have been blessed as a nation. Other cultures have also endured suffering such as African Americans and Indians to name a few. My point in sharing this analogy is to encourage you in your suffering. Hold on to God's promises because they will manifest at the appointed time. Remember, God has a purpose for your pain.

My definition of perseverance is "undeterred ability to keep moving amid difficult circumstances."

The Reward of Suffering

A powerful revelation regarding suffering is found in Romans 5: 3-5: "Not only so, but we also glory in our sufferings, because we know that suffering produces perseverance; perseverance, character; and character, hope. And hope does not put us to shame, because God's love has been poured out into our hearts through the Holy Spirit, who has been given to us"(NIV). This passage conveys three virtues—perseverance, character, and hope—that God will develop through your suffering. Let's take a close look at these virtues individually.

Perseverance

We shared insight regarding perseverance in Chapter 2. Webster's Dictionary defines perseverance as persistence in doing something despite of difficulty or delay. My definition of perseverance is "undeterred ability to keep moving amid difficult circumstances." God's word is your motivation because His word is true and will not return unto Him void. Hannah was unaware that God was birthing something great out of her. God seldom reveals the full picture of

His purpose in our lives. However, if you continue to trust Him no matter what, you will observe His plans unfolding in your life.

I was a caregiver for my mother as she endured Alzheimer's. I had relocated to Arkansas from Dallas in Spring 2017 to assist my siblings who lived near our mother. I thank God for the eight children my mother had. Four of us were able to alter our lives to provide care for her near and at the end of her life.

I could not embrace the reality that my mother was afflicted with this disease. My mother was a prayer warrior. She assisted me when I began my prayer ministry Apostolic House of Prayer (AHOP) in 2012. She was faithful on the prayer line for a year. During her suffering, I had to persevere and not allow the circumstance of her failing health to consume me. My father had died five years earlier as a result of several medical complications. My mother had been his steadfast, primary caregiver. God spoke to me and said, *"do not to try to figure out everything; trust in my Sovereignty."*

It was God's purpose for me to be there because my brothers could only give Mother limited amount of care. She needed the aid of my sister and me regarding more sensitive and personal aspects. My siblings and I watched Mother take her last breath August 24, 2017. I thank God that I was with her during her time of suffering! Her suffering ended with her last breath on earth and her healing began with her first breath in Heaven! She is now in the presence of the Lord! I thank God that I was led by His Spirit to complete the assignment with my mother. It was an assignment that led me to persevere in the midst of an unforeseen circumstance.

During this difficult time, I persisted in my personal walk with God. I later moved back to Dallas and began my own life again. I had remained focused during my time with my ailing mother. Remaining focused is essential when facing difficult situations.

Character

I remind people that you do not just want to have a "good character," but a "God character." Your character defines the real you! People will judge you on how you live, not by what you say.

> *People will judge you on how you live, not by what you say.*

If you claim to be a Christian, evidence in your life should validate this truth. The Bible has much to say about one's character.

Let's look at Proverbs 22:1 from the Message Bible: "sterling reputation is better than striking it rich; a gracious spirit is better than money in the bank."

This is a powerful truth! Your reputation is better than money! Your reputation is your character!

I pray and decree every day that I have a good name when others speak of me or hear of me.

When people hear your name, what words come to their mind that describes you? This is a great question!

Ponder on it for a moment. When people hear my name, the words I believe they hear are "full of integrity, faithful, transparent, and chaste," just to name a few. Pain and suffering are emotions that God uses to make a better you! His objective is to get you transformed into His image!

This is my daily prayer: "Lord, make me look like you!" He told us in Romans 12:1 to "be ye transformed by the renewing of your mind." As we study and apply God's word to our lives, we begin to walk in the image of God. I thank God for this truth that was revealed to me many years ago.

Many believers in the church are saved but have not experienced *transformation.* That is why the world is so confused! Why? Because Christians continue to do the same things that unbelievers do while confessing to be Jesus followers.

The Bible speaks of these believers as being "carnal." They are still "living in the flesh" as they did before they were saved. A carnal Christian has not totally surrendered their life unto the Lord. They still have an appetite for the world. I pray that you do not fall into this category and that God will give you a hunger and thirst for Him. When you hunger and thirst after God you can flourish as a Christian.

It is the Lord's purpose to develop character within us. "The crucible for silver and the furnace for gold, but the LORD tests the heart" (Proverbs 17:3).

Character in the believer is a consistent manifestation of Jesus in their life. When your character looks like Jesus, it will display the light of God in your heart—a light that speaks to a dark world. Christians are supposed to be the light of the world. If our light is hidden, it is hidden to those who are perishing. We are called to shine our lights; not to hide them under a bushel!

A scripture that many children learned at an early age is John 3:16: "For God so loved the world, that he gave his only begotten Son, that whosoever believeth in him should not perish, but have everlasting life." Saving souls should be the priority of every Christian. If our character is sending mixed messages, we will not be able to fulfill the charge through the Great Commission in Matthew 28:19-20.

Hope

The last virtue we will observe that God develops through your suffering is hope. What is hope? It is defined as a feeling of expectation and desire for a certain thing to happen. Hope is a virtue that is absent in our world today because many people do not have clarity regarding how to receive hope.

Suicide is a result of someone without hope. Unbelievers can experience the same suffering as Christians; however, one thing that we have available to us is hope. Who is the source of our hope? Let's review Romans 15:13, "Now the God of hope fill you with all joy and peace in believing, that ye may abound in hope, through the power of the Holy Ghost."

Hallelujah! This scripture reveals that we can abound in hope through the power of the Holy Ghost. As we observe all the activities that are happening in our world, it appears that we live in a world without hope. Crime has escalated. Moral values have declined. Where there is no fear of God, you can expect lawlessness. Matthew 24:12 reveals this truth: "And because lawlessness will be increased, the love of many will grow cold."

In the midst of the lawlessness there is a "remnant." We are the remnant, God's church. We are the ones who will persevere no matter what. We must continue to produce the hope that will manifest the promises of God. We must continue to hope for our nation.

We must continue to
produce the hope that will
manifest the promises of God.

We must pray that our nation will line up with God's word. Let's believe the words of this prayer and, together, say it aloud:

Father, I come to you and ask that you keep my hope alive. In the midst of my suffering I decree that I will not lose hope. I submit my dreams, vision, family, ministry, and business to YOU and ask that your purpose and plans prevail in them. Thank you, Lord, for being my source of hope and strength and I rest in you as you demonstrate your sovereignty in my life.
In Jesus' Name, I pray. Amen!"

Chapter 4: Suffering in Silence
Application for My Life

1. Is suffering a part of life? ___Yes ___No

2. What is the Webster's Dictionary definition of suffering?

3. What scripture encourages us not to give place (opportunity) to the devil?

4. Can you name a time when you gave place to the devil? ___Yes __ No

5. What was the opportunity you presented to the devil?

6. What are three rewards of suffering?

7. Why is your character important to God?

8. Who is the source of our hope?

Answers to Life Application Questions

1.

2.

3.

4.

5.

6.

7.

8.

Chapter 5

Making and Honoring a Vow

We have all been guilty of making a vow and not honoring it. Don't tell me I'm the only one (lol)! I pray for people all the time and have often heard the following: "Lord if you bless me with a car, I will go to church." Then, when they get the car, they forget about the promise that they made to God. Here's another vow that I have heard people make: "Lord if you bless me with a job, I will be faithful in paying my tithes." After the person gets the job, by the time the bills are paid and the shopping spree is over, there is nothing left for the tithe! Get the picture?

I want you to understand the severity of making a vow and why we cannot take it lightly. What does the Bible say about making a vow? I am glad you asked that question! Let's observe Numbers 30:1,2:

> *And Moses spake unto the heads of the tribes concerning the children of Israel, saying, This is the thing which the LORD hath commanded.*
>
> *If a man vow a vow unto the LORD or swear an oath to bind his soul with a bond; he shall not break his word, he shall do according to all that proceedeth out of his mouth.*

The words vow and pledge are interchangeable; both mean to make a solemn promise. When you make a promise, you are giving your word that you have made a commitment to do something.

The above scriptures admonish us to keep every vow we make unto the Lord; we are not to break our promise. My point in sharing this passage is to ensure that you do not make a vow just to make one, but to do it with purpose and understanding. The Word says in Ecclesiastes 5:5, "*It is better not to make a vow than to make one and not fulfill it.*"

The Power of a Vow

People generally make a vow unto the Lord when they are in trouble or faced with difficult circumstances. Let's observe the first recorded vow made to God in the Bible. In Genesis 28:20-22 Jacob, the son of Isaac vowed:

> *Then Jacob made a vow, saying, If God will be with me and will watch over me on this journey I am taking and will give me food to eat and clothes to wear* [21] *so that I return safely to my father's household, then the LORD will be my God* [22] *and this stone that I have set up as a pillar will be God's house, and of all that you give me I will give you a tenth.*"

What was going on in Jacob's life that prompted him to present this vow unto the Lord? To gain insight into Jacob's circumstance we would have to read Genesis Chapter 27; I would encourage you to do so when you have a moment. Here is a brief explanation as to why Jacob made the vow. Jacob was one of the twins born to Isaac and Rebekah; the other was Esau. At birth Jacob grabbed Esau's heel as he was exiting the birth canal, nonetheless Esau came out first, and was the firstborn.

It was the custom in that place and era that the birthright and blessing belonged to the firstborn. Jacob, however, found a way of stealing Esau's birthright. Through deception and lies and the manipulation of his mother, Jacob also stole Esau's blessing. Esau was truly angry and threatened to kill Jacob. Rebekah suggested that Jacob flee to his uncle Laban's home. Jacob was a man on the run and hid in caves before making it to his destination.

As you continue to read through the book of Genesis, you will see that Jacob was faithful to his vow, and God changed the heart of his brother Esau and they were reconciled.

Similarly, Hannah found herself in distress. In her desperation for a son, she made a vow unto the Lord. 1 Samuel 1:10,11 tells us:

> [10]*And she was in bitterness of soul, and prayed unto the* LORD, *and wept sore.* [11] *And she vowed a vow, and said, O* LORD *of hosts, if thou wilt indeed look on the affliction of thine handmaid, and remember me, and not forget thine handmaid, but wilt give unto thine handmaid a man child, then I will give him unto the* LORD *all the days of his life, and there shall no razor come upon his head.*

I want to look at three areas where you will be challenged when you make a vow:

- **Accountability** — *The fact or condition of being accountable, responsibility.* When you make the vow, you will be held responsible to honor the vow. Simply stated, accountability is being responsible for your actions. Remember, making a vow is like making a promise. How many times have people promised to do something for you and did not honor that promise? How did that make you feel? Have you ever made a promise, but it was delayed, or you did not honor the promise? I believe we all have been guilty of this act. God expects us to be accountable (Romans 14:2).

- **Integrity**—There was a generation that not only understood the importance of the spoken word but demonstrated it in their lives. I remember my father drilling into us that, "your word is your bond." More than likely you have also heard this statement. Proverbs 10:9 says Whoever walks in integrity walks securely, but whoever takes crooked paths will be found out. (NIV) Dishonesty will be exposed at the opportune time. Every believer should develop the attribute of integrity.

- **Humility** — You are probably wondering by now what role humility plays in fulfilling a vow. Humility is the quality of being humble. If an unforeseen circumstance occurs in your life that deters you from fulfilling your vow, you need to revise your plan. The spirit of pride will manifest if you do not embrace the spirit of humility. Pride will tell you not to worry about anything and to just keep moving forward. Here is where you need to go before the Lord with a contrite heart in humility and ask Him for guidance.

The Vow Honored

There is a lesson to learn from the vow that Hannah made unto the Lord. It is evident that her perspective had changed because it was not about her having a son. She wanted her son's life to have purpose. Hannah was not cognizant that God had a purpose for her son because she was so consumed with her barrenness. She could not see beyond her circumstance.

One advantage that we have over Hannah as believers under the New Covenant is that we have direct access to God through the blood shed by Christ on the Cross and the power of the Holy Spirit. As we yield to Him daily, we can speak to our circumstance by speaking the Word of God over it. Remember we were created to be *speaking spirits.* Proverbs 18:21 says that death and life are in the power of the tongue. The Kingdom of God operates through the spoken word. What we want from the Kingdom we must speak into existence!

The Kingdom of God operates through the spoken word. What we want from the Kingdom we must speak into existence!

As you continue to read Hannah's story, you will see that not only did she make a vow, she was committed to it and honored it. Let's face it; Hannah made a great sacrifice! What mother would give up her child after birth? That's a hard task, but Hannah did not succumb to her emotions; instead, she remembered her vow and kept her word. Thus, Hannah agreed that her son would serve the Lord perpetually as a Nazirite. The word *Nazarite* means *to be consecrated or set apart.* If you read the entire chapter of Numbers 6 you will gain insight into the *Nazarite Law of Separation.* However, I am going to provide a summary for you. The purpose of the vow of the Nazirite was to express one's special desire to draw close to God and to separate one's self from the comforts and pleasures of this world. I admonish you to read the vow in its entirety in Numbers 6 to gain more insight.

1. The Nazirite was forbidden to eat or drink anything from the grape vine; this was a form of self-denial connected with the idea of a special consecration to God.

2. No razor shall come upon his head: The hair was to be allowed to grow all during the period of the vow, and

then cut at the conclusion of the vow. This was a way of outwardly demonstrating to the world that this man or woman was under a special vow.

What a great lesson we can learn from Hannah, a mother who dedicated her child unto the Lord immediately after birth! Only a mother could understand how difficult this must have been, but God rewarded Hannah for her faithfulness. Similarly, He will reward you and me, as we are steadfast to honor and trust Him. Remember making a vow is serious and it challenges your integrity when you do not honor it!

Chapter 5: Making and Honoring A Vow
Application for My Life

1. After reading chapter 5, what is your perception of the word *vow*?

2. Why did Hannah make a vow?

3. What does Ecclesiastes 5:5 says about making a vow?

4. What passage of Scripture reveals the first vow made in the Bible?

5. What three areas are we challenged in when we make a vow?

6. How was Hannah committed to her vow?

7. What insights have you learned that have helped you understand the severity of making a vow?

Answers to Life Application Questions

1.

2.

3.

4.

5.

6.

7.

Chapter 6

The Power of Travail

Hannah had to wake up every morning and gaze upon Peninnah and her children while she carried an empty womb. She lost her appetite and strength as she endured the harassment of her adversary. Hannah did not realize that God's purpose for closing her womb was about to manifest.

I want us to look closely at the word *travail*, an expression that is often used in the body of Christ. *Webster's Dictionary* defines *travail* as follows: *work, especially of a painful or* difficult nature. 2: Agony, torment; toil.

To travail is to be troubled, sorrowful, in agony, intense pain or distress.

To travail is to be troubled, sorrowful, in agony, intense pain or distress.

Travail is hard work; it is not a comfortable experience! While many intercessors understand the term, others have misconstrued it. I always ask God to give me revelation and understanding on whatever I experience in prayer. I certainly want to teach by revelation, and not reiterate what I hear others saying. When you do not have a clear perception of something, you engage in it from your emotions and not by the Spirit of God. I have seen some abnormal things happen at prayer gatherings that people call travail. I knew by the Spirit, however, that it was not travail and did not engage in it.

It is imperative to note that the words *travail*, and *childbirth* are interchangeable. Several years ago, I participated as a prayer leader at a corporate prayer gathering at a church in Houston, Texas. Each prayer leader had a different prayer focus to pray over. There were other intercessors gathered around the altar as we prayed. Suddenly one of the intercessors began screaming out loud and holding her stomach. A couple of intercessors formed a circle around her. She later put her hand on her stomach and started breathing like she was having a baby. It became a distraction until someone in authority had to break up the circle. What was wrong with this picture? The Holy Spirit does not act unseemly. He does not bring confusion. This is a perfect example of someone acting out of their emotions. The soul realm (flesh) will cause you to be dramatic and draw attention to yourself.

What does the Bible say about *travail*? Here are a few scriptures that reference the word:

Psalm 48:6 - *Panic seized them there, anguish, as of a woman in childbirth.*

Isaiah 66:8 - *Who hath heard such a thing? who hath seen such things? Shall the earth be made to bring forth in one day? or shall a nation be born at once? for as soon as Zion travailed, she brought forth her children.*

John 16:21 - *A woman when she is in travail hath sorrow, because her hour is come: but as soon as she is delivered of the child, she remembered no more the anguish, for joy that a man is born into the world.*

We can see from the above Scripture passages that there are several words associated with travail, including *anguish, agony, and pain*. All these synonyms were evident in Hannah's cry of travail and are associated with childbirth.

Pushed into Purpose

It was the agonizing pain of barrenness and the perpetual emotional abuse that Hannah experienced from her rival that pushed her into a position of travail. It was a cry of brokenness and desperation! Have you ever been there? I know that I have! It is a place where you feel abandoned, but God is there. Jesus has experienced this place as well. When the soldiers came to arrest Jesus in the garden, all his disciples fled (Mark 14:50). Another occasion was while He was on the Cross; with the sins of the world upon Him, he felt forsaken. Mark 15:34 expresses this truth: *"And at three in the afternoon Jesus cried out in a loud voice, "Eloi, Eloi, lema sabachthani?" (which means "My God, my God, why have you forsaken me?").*

According to Hebrews 13:5, God promises to never leave us or forsake us. We can stand on this truth! I am going to share insight on the process of travail from two perspectives, the natural and spiritual. In the case of *natural childbirth*, some women choose to give birth using no medications at all, relying instead on techniques such as relaxation and controlled breathing to alleviate and lessen pain. With *natural childbirth*, the mother is in control of her body, usually with a labor assistant (midwife) gently guiding and supporting her through the stages of labor.

In the natural, before the baby comes out, the water must break. Simultaneously, the mother experiences pain which accompanies the contractions. The labor pains are often excruciating. To alleviate this acute distress, women are often given the option of taking pain killing medication. The most popular form of medicating the pain is through an *epidural*. While she is in the labor room the doctor and his team are telling her to push. Once the cervix has dilated to 10 cm, it could take about an hour or two of pushing before the baby is born; the more power she places behind the push, the sooner the baby will come out.

> *God is using your pain, suffering, and trials to push you in position to birth out what He has purposed for you.*

It is the same process in the *spiritual realm*. Essentially, God is using your pain, suffering, and trials to push you in position to birth out what He has purposed for you. The reality is you never know what is down on the inside of YOU until you are overwhelmed with pressure! PUSH is the acronym associated with *Pray Until Something Happens*. I can attest to being under such intense pressure on several occasions in my life that I knew I was getting ready to deliver! However, there were other times when my circumstances were so difficult that it appeared that my visions and dreams were being aborted. But thank God for the midwives in my life that prayed me through.

When you sow seeds of intercession, you will reap a harvest of intercession! I pray that your dreams and visions manifest in their fullness. I come against every spirit that has been sent to abort the visions and dreams that are down on the inside of you! I decree and declare that *no weapon formed against you shall prosper* (Isaiah 54:17)! This is a promise that every believer can activate!

The Birthing Process

In the case of Hannah, she did not have a team cheering her on. She did not have a midwife or medication to alleviate her pain.

Hannah had a relationship with Yahweh, and she trusted Him for divine intervention. Remember, it was God that closed Hannah's womb.

Is it not just like God to create a circumstance to reveal His Glory? There are some circumstances that we create because of our disobedience; even in those situations, however, God extends His mercy towards us.

I shared earlier in this book that our society is faced with some hard times due to the Coronavirus pandemic. God did not create this pandemic, but He is using it to reveal His Glory.

During this time of isolation, writer's block has been eradicated off my life and I am able to write. God used this time of isolation to put me in position to birth three books!

I am doing what I love and simultaneously helping others get their books published! On the eve of Passover, I birthed a Writing Class I titled, "Manifest Your Book Now."

Through the class, I provided free coaching to emerging authors who became members of the group that I created on Facebook. I shared strategies and principles on how to get your book published within 90 days. I presented weekly challenges to these emerging authors and those who implemented these strategies saw their writing skills come to life.

God used me as a midwife to help them birth their book! It was my obedience to the voice of God that caused me to be a blessing to others.

Several years ago, Mike Murdock, a prominent teacher on scriptural wealth principles, released the following quote:

"What you make happen for others God will make happen for you." In other words, *what you sow into another person's life God will release into yours!* This truth became a reality in my life! I gained clients from the coaching classes; it was evident that they were on schedule to publish their books by July 31, 2020 and were prepared for the upcoming book signing on August 29, 2020.

> *What you make happen for others God will make happen for you.*

Let's use our spiritual imagination as we observe the power of travail manifesting through Hannah. Hannah wept until she had no more tears; we could say that her water had broken. She was under the pressure of anguish, grief, and pain, and these elements were her contractions. She identifies her emotional status in 1 Samuel 1:12-18, which reads:

> [12] *And it came to pass, as she continued praying before the* Lord, *that Eli marked her mouth.*

> [13] *Now Hannah, she spake in her heart; only her lips moved, but her voice was not heard: therefore, Eli thought she had been drunken.*

> [14] *And Eli said unto her, how long wilt thou be drunken? put away thy wine from thee.*

> [15] *And Hannah answered and said, No, my lord, I am a woman of a sorrowful spirit: I have drunk neither wine nor strong drink but have poured out my soul before the* Lord.

[16] *Count not thine handmaid for a daughter of Belial: for out of the abundance of my complaint and grief have I spoken hitherto.*

[17] *Then Eli answered and said, Go in peace: and the God of Israel grant thee thy petition that thou hast asked of him.*

[18] *And she said, Let thine handmaid find grace in thy sight. So the woman went her way, and did eat, and her countenance was no more sad.*

There are times in our lives when we will be faced with circumstances that we have no control over. We must continue to trust God!

In addition to her being in despair, Hannah was wrongly accused by Eli, who alleged that she was drunk with wine. She was not offended and clarified that she was not a daughter of Belial. The Hebrew word for *Belial* is translated *wickedness* or *worthlessness*; certainly, she did not want to be put in that category! Rather, Hannah described her condition as being a woman of a sorrowful spirit. The Hebrew word for *sorrowful* means *to be heavy; mournful; unhappy.*

Hannah was heartbroken because she was faced with a circumstance that she had no control over. There are times in our lives when we will be faced with circumstances that we have no control over. We must continue to trust God! Look what Hannah was faced with:

- She was in a polygamous marriage
- She was barren
- She was harassed daily by Peninnah

This would be the last time that Hannah would journey to Shiloh regarding this issue; she had pressed her way into the presence of God! Hannah knew that it was going to take a supernatural move of God for her to conceive, and so she poured out her soul unto the Lord. Upon the completion of her intercession, Eli declared to Hannah that she could go on her way because God has answered her prayer! When Hannah got up her countenance had changed. The sorrowful spirit had been eradicated!

To hear her testimony in the fullness you would have to read 1 Samuel Chapter 2, where we see Hannah rejoicing in the Lord through a prophetic song. She is making a joyful noise unto the Lord because she is happy! This is the end result of travail. In the natural, when the baby is born, the woman is no longer sad or experiencing pain. When the nurse brings the child to her, she is happy!

If what you are experiencing right now is causing you despair, you are in the right place to give birth to what God has put on the inside of you! I call that SEED to **come forth, In Jesus Name!**

Chapter 6 Assessment: The Power of Travail
Application for My Life

1. Who was Hannah's number one enemy?

2. What is Webster's definition of the word "travail?'

3. What happens when you try to engage travail without knowledge?

4. PUSH is the acronym for _____
   _____.

5. What two scripture references reveal Jesus experiencing the agonizing pain of travail?

6. What did Hannah mean when she said, "I am a woman of a sorrowful spirit?"

7. What happened after Hannah poured out her soul unto the Lord?

Answers to Life Application Questions

1.

2.

3.

4.

5.

6.

7.

Manifestation of the Promise

As we continue to observe 1 Samuel Chapter 1, we learn that Hannah's request was not only heard, but God *answered* her prayer. That is the goal! We do not want God just to hear us; we want Him to respond with a "yes."! Of course, a "yes" answer is not always the case. Sometime God will respond with a "wait" or a "no." Whenever God responds with "no" we should not be dismayed. We must remember that He knows what is best for us and he can see the big picture of our lives.

Sometimes when we pray and our motives do not line up with His word, He will decline our request. The passage in James 4:3 reveals this truth: "You ask and do not receive, because you ask amiss, that you may spend it on your pleasures." If we want God to answer our prayers, our motives must be pure and if they are, they will line up with the will and plan of God. Thank God that Hannah did not lose hope in her barrenness.

Oftentimes we find ourselves faced with circumstances that contradict God's Word, but we must not be moved by what we see in the *natural.* Conversely, we must cling to the truth that God works in the *supernatural* and his timeline is not like ours!

In addition, the Bible says that what we see is *temporary* but those things that we cannot see are *eternal.* We must continue to stand on the promises with confidence that God is going to honor His word. Hannah waited for the promise to manifest.

What does the Bible say about waiting on the promise? Let us observe these scriptures:

Isaiah 40:31: But they who *wait* for the LORD shall renew their strength; they shall mount up with wings like eagles; they shall run and not be weary; they shall walk and not faint.

Psalm 27:14: *Wait* on the LORD: be of good courage, and he shall strengthen thine heart: *wait*, I say, on the LORD.

I can attest that waiting is sometimes difficult, but it is something that we must endure. I want to draw your attention to 1 Samuel 1:17: "Then Eli answered and said, Go in peace: and the God of Israel grant thee thy petition that thou hast asked of him."

After Eli got the revelation that Hannah was not drunk as he perceived in verse 16, he was able to respond to her. It is imperative to note that Eli's presence at Shiloh played a vital role in Hannah's prayer being answered. He was not like his sons who did not fear God and did wickedness in His sight. Eli was a high priest of Shiloh who interceded for Hannah and blessed her. Jesus is our high priest and the word declares that he lives to make intercession for us. (Romans 8:34) That's right, my friend! Jesus is at the right hand of the father praying for you right now! You are not alone. Jesus promises to never leave us nor forsake us. Sometimes it may feel as if He is not in the storm with us, but He is! That's good news! In the interim, God will give you divine strategies to help you overcome every obstacle that attempts to deter the promise.

It is imperative that you do not become weary in your waiting. I know patience is not a virtue that we want to embrace, but it is certainly going to manifest while you are waiting on the promises!

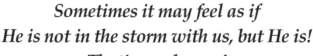

Sometimes it may feel as if He is not in the storm with us, but He is! That's good news!

Strategies to Implement While Waiting on the Promise

Let's look at some strategies to implement while waiting on the manifestation of the promise:

1. Continue in prayer. Do not stop praying! You will experience complete joy when you began to intercede for others! Your focus will shift as you pray for other families, your community, and your nation. The word encourages us to bear the burden of one another. (Galatians 6:2) I enjoy applying this scripture because I am strengthened in my inner man as I intercede for others. The power of God began to destroy every yoke in my life as well as the people that I am interceding for. I want to encourage you today to pick up the burden of your brethren while you are waiting for the manifestation of the promise!

2. Continue in worship. Worship is a lifestyle; it is not a Sunday experience! We must enter the presence of God daily. In His presence is the fullness of joy! I cannot imagine a day without worship. I also pray in tongues. Employing this strategy releases the power that is needed to overcome the enemy. He is after everything that looks like God. That is, you and me! One of my favorite scriptures is in Ephesians 6:10-11, which reads: Finally, be strong in the Lord, and his mighty power; Put on the full armor of God so that you can take your stand against the devil schemes. (NIV) The devil has devised a plan for you and me. If we apply the above scripture, we can overthrow the plans of our enemy.

3. Continue studying the word of God. I cannot emphasize the severity of you spending time studying the word. We

are living in an age where people have itching ears, and everybody is looking for a word. Many are not getting the revelation of studying the word of God and making it priority!

Our society is full of people with false hope. But those who are citizens of the kingdom continue to hope in Christ. Psalms 33:20-22 says: Our soul waiteth for the Lord: he is our help and our shield. For our heart shall rejoice in him because we have trusted in his holy name. Let thy mercy, O Lord, be upon us, according as we hope in thee." Keep hope alive! The promises will MANIFEST! God is not man that He should lie. His promises are yes and AMEN!

Four Benefits of Waiting

If someone would have told me that "waiting is a process," I would have endured many trails and tests differently. Waiting is indeed a lost discipline in the body of Christ. Only those who wait on the manifestation of the promises will reap the benefit of this discipline.

Let us observe Isaiah 40:31 that identifies benefits afforded to us as we wait: "They that wait upon the Lord shall renew their strength; they shall mount up with wings as eagles; they shall run, and not be weary; and they shall walk, and not faint."

Benefit 1 – Our strength is renewed. There are times when we are going through difficult trials that can literally squeeze the very life out of us. No matter what, we must continue to confess the Word of God. Psalm 27:1 reads: "The Lord is my light and my salvation. Who shall I fear; He is the strength of my life. Whom shall I be afraid?

Did you catch that promise? He is *the strength of my life.* That indicates when He is in control of my life, I can draw strength from

Him. Many believers allow their circumstances to consume them. They forget that God is greater than their circumstances.

Benefit 2 – We will mount up with wings as eagles. This is a figure of speech that implies that those who remain faithful and put their trust in God will overcome the obstacles of life. History conveys to us that Israel was in a place of oppression under the Assyrian captivity. Isaiah is prophesying and encouraging the Israelites not to lose hope in the midst of oppression.

> *When we remain focused on the promises of God, we will not become weary. . . the promises of God are "yes and amen."*

Sometimes we must be reminded that the same God that brought you out on yesterday is going to bring you out today! God brought them out of Egypt, and He promised to bring them out of this captivity. God uses the eagle to describe the life of those who wait with expectation. The eagles spread their wings and they soar high! With their wings spread, they plunder fearlessly into the storm.

Benefit 3 – We shall run and not grow weary. During our waiting, we must continue to stay focused on what we are waiting on. When you think of the word "run" what comes to mind? If you are running that means that you are moving.

The Hebrew word run means "to bring or move quickly." When we remain focused on the promises of God, we will not become weary. We know that the promises of God are "yes and amen," according to the scriptures (2 Corinthians 1:20). The word weary means "to become tired." I minister to believers all the time who express to me that they are just tired. Tired of waiting and tired of persevering! We must take on the stance of David and encourage ourselves in the Lord. David was in a difficult situation where his back was up against the wall. He did not know what to do. He had no option but to trust God!

The scripture reveals that David inquired of the Lord and received instructions and strategies as to how to proceed. Let us observe 1 Samuel 30:6-8: "And David was greatly distressed; for the people spake of stoning him, because the soul of all the people was grieved, every man for his sons and for his daughters: but David encouraged himself in the Lord his God.

"And David said to Abiathar the priest, Ahimelech's son, I pray thee, bring me hither the ephod. And Abiathar brought thither the ephod to David. And David enquired at the Lord, saying, Shall I pursue after this troop? Shall I overtake them? And he answered him, Pursue: for thou shalt surely overtake them, and without fail recover all."

David eradicated his enemies the Amalekites because he followed God's instructions. He gained strength from God and he was encouraged. He was ready to face the next giant!

We can learn from David by inquiring of the Lord when we are faced with difficult trials and test. When we get in His presence, we will receive clarity and direction; but most of all we will gain strength! The Bible declares that the joy of the Lord is our strength.

Benefit 4 – We shall walk and not faint. The last benefit of waiting encourages us to walk and not faint. If we are walking that is an indication that we are still standing. The word challenges us to stand and having done all to stand, to continue standing! (Ephesians 6:13) When we get knocked down, we get back up! If we keep our eyes on Jesus, we will not faint. To faint implies giving up. I do not know about you, but I have come to far to give up! I have been through too much. I have seen too much. I encourage you to hold on because the PROMISE is going to MANIFEST!

Chapter 7:Manifestation of the Promise
Application for My Life

1. Why is it imperative to have pure motives when we pray?

2. What promise did God manifest for Hannah?

3. What are three ways God responds to our request?

4. Name a strategy we can implement while waiting on the promise.

5. What are four benefits of waiting on the promise?

Answers to Life Application Questions

1.

2.

3.

4.

5.

6.

Chapter 8

Favor is Your Kingdom Portion

A popular word in Christian circles today is *favor*. Believers often use this term when greeting one another. For example, a typical interaction between Church goers might be as follows:

"How are you doing?"

"I am blessed and highly *favored* of the Lord!"

This phrase has become a cliché. Most believers do not really know what it means to be favored by God. His favor, or grace, is the divine ability to do something which is humanly impossible.

God's favor, or grace, is the divine ability to do something which is humanly impossible.

God uses ordinary people, but because of His favor, these people become extraordinary as they fulfill His purpose. We see a manifestation of this truth in Luke 1:28, where an angel comes to Mary and conveys these words: *"And the angel came in unto her, and said, Hail, thou that art highly favored, the Lord is with thee: blessed art thou among women."*

Mary was an ordinary woman, but God chose her to carry His seed and give birth to *His Only Begotten Son*. Out of the myriad of women in the world God could have chosen, He chose Mary! What did Mary do to earn this favor? Nothing! You cannot work for the favor of God! We could say that God's *amazing grace* was presented to Mary; God gave her more than what she asked for or deserved! Now let's get back to Hannah.

> **When you obey the voice of God, the favor of God is released upon you and your seed!**

Let me recap the definition of *Hannah*. Her name means *favor* or *grace*. This characterization is certainly manifested in her life. We shared in *Chapter 2* how she presented a specific request unto the Lord, which was for Yahweh to bless her with a male child. God honored her request and He did much more!

As we read 1 Samuel 2 verses 18-21, we see that the Lord blessed Hannah with several children in addition to Samuel. Scripture reveals that while Samuel was a child, Elkanah and Hannah would go up to Shiloh to present their annual sacrifice. Hannah made a special garment for Samuel, called an *ephod*. Samuel wore the ephod as he ministered unto the Lord.

As you follow the lineage of Hannah in Scripture, you will see that favor was not only on Hannah, but on her seed as well. Hannah did not allow her barrenness to affect her relationship with God; she could have gotten angry with Him and blamed God for closing her womb. Oftentimes, this is what we do as believers. We blame God for our pain and sufferings instead of seeking His purpose for allowing it in our lives. When you obey the voice of God, the favor of God is released upon you and your seed!

The Overflow

The Holy Scriptures reveal to us that Eli the priest declared a blessing upon Hannah, after which the Lord remembered her again. Let's read 1 Samuel 2, verses 20 and 21:

And Eli blessed Elkanah and his wife, and said, The Lord gives thee seed of this woman for the loan which is lent to the Lord. And they went unto their own home. And the Lord visited Hannah, so that she conceived, and bare three sons and two daughters. And the child Samuel grew before the Lord.

According to the above passage of Scriptures, Hannah had a total of six children. How awesome is that! A woman that was once barren is now walking in the overflow! This is what the favor of God looks like. I can attest to the favor of God upon my life. I have walked through some doors that opened for me because of the favor of God. What does the Bible say about the favor of God? Here are a few Scriptures:

Psalms 5:12 – *For thou, Lord will bless the righteous; with favor will thou compass him as with a shield.*

Psalms 84:11 - *For the Lord God is a sun and shield: the Lord will give grace and glory: no good thing will he withhold from them that walk uprightly.*

Romans 6:14 – *For sin will have no dominion over you, since you are not under law but under grace.*

Hebrews 4:16 - *Let us therefore come boldly unto the throne of grace, that we may obtain mercy, and find grace to help in time of need.*

I shared scriptures from both the Old and New Testaments so that you might gain insight regarding the Hebrew and Greek definition of the word favor. Wherever you see the word *grace*, it is interpreted as *unmerited favor.* Simply put, grace is *an undeserved, unworked for favor from God to mankind.* I thank God for the unmerited favor that He has demonstrated in my life, as revealed in the following testimony. May it bless you tremendously.

My Personal Testimony

In August of 2019 I relocated from Houston, Texas to move closer to my children in Arlington, Texas for a season. As I settled into my new location, I began to encounter excruciating pain in my abdomen. I was sure the pain was due to gallstones since I had been diagnosed with them in March of 2018 after my visit to the Emergency Room. The physician there suggested getting my gallbladder removed, but I declined.

On October 1, 2019 I drove to the emergency room due to the pain in my abdomen. I told the doctor that I knew my pain was due to gallstones, but they insisted on doing another ultrasound. They found multiple gallstones which were not infectious.

They released me and told me to just wait and see if they would pass I took some natural remedies hoping that the gallstones would dissolve, but they did not. On October 9, 2019, a pain that I had never encountered before exploded in my left side, sending me straight to the floor. I became nauseous and dragged myself to the bathroom to throw up. I kept throwing up and feeling dizzy; I asked the Lord what to do. I heard the Spirit say, "Call 911."

I called 911 and began to tell the dispatcher what was going on. She asked me if I had fallen; I replied that I had not. She then encouraged me to remain calm; the ambulance was on the way. After the ambulance arrived and took all my vitals, I was taken to the nearest hospital, called *Medical City Arlington*. You know the routine. They put me on IV and began to take all kinds of tests, ranging from an EKG, to X-rays, and ultrasounds. They discovered that there was a kidney stone blocked in or around my ureter. For you to have a clear understanding of what I am communicating, I have provided some medical terminology from the Google site:

Ureteral stones are kidney stones that have become stuck in one or both ureters (the tubes that carry urine from the kidneys to the bladder). If the stone is large enough, it can block the flow of urine from the kidney to the bladder. This blockage can cause severe pain.

The pain was excruciating; I am so glad that I obeyed God and called 911. I prayed and asked God to favor me with the hospital staff. God did just what I requested. The doctor told me that they needed to remove the stone and that it would be a minor procedure, which he explained to me; I was comforted knowing that I was not having open surgery. The medical personnel then went in and removed the stone with a laser.

I was treated with supreme care. It was evident that the favor of God was upon me by the services that were provided by the staff. I checked in on October 9th and the procedure was performed on the 11th. I remember the Anesthesiologist coming into the room and telling me what was going to happen. She explained that after she had administered the medicine, I would not remember anything.

I woke up in recovery and the pain had dissipated. They took me back upstairs to my room and I began to pray in the Spirit in my mind. I was so grateful to God that this was over. I was discharged on October 12th. I had to cancel my trip to New York that I had previously planned with my children. We were all going to surprise my granddaughter for her 16th birthday with this trip. My children were reluctant to proceed with the trip due to this unforeseen circumstance, but I encouraged them to go and have fun.

I remember the intake counselor coming into my room on the day of my discharge, asking me whether I needed financial assistance; my medical insurance had been terminated after my relocation. I was still under the influence of pain medication and was not coherent; I was unable to respond to any of her questions. As I prepared to go home, all I could do was lay in bed for a moment and focus on the grace of God. The scripture that came to mind was 2 Corinthians 12:9, which says, And he said unto me, My grace is sufficient for thee: for my strength is made perfect in weakness. Most gladly therefore will I rather glory in my infirmities, that the power of Christ may rest upon me." Thank God for the manifestation of his grace! "No matter what you are going through you need to know that God's grace is sufficient and will carry you through."

> *No matter what you are going through you need to know that God's grace is sufficient and will carry you through.*

One of my friends came to pick me up from the hospital and take me home. Time progressed, and day by day, the Lord was renewing my strength. I finally got my medical bill in the mail. When I opened it, I could not believe what I saw; the total cost was **$94,000!** I knew that it was going to be high, but I had no idea that it would be that high! I prayed and inquired of God as to what I should do; the Lord brought back to my remembrance what the administrative counselor had communicated regarding financial assistance. I called and requested an application. After it was mailed to me, I completed it and made copies of all the supporting documents that needed to accompany the application.

When I called the hospital to verify the address to which I should send the document, the clerk asked me for my account number. After receiving the account number, she reviewed my account and told me that the bill had already been paid in full.

Stunned, I said, "Are you sure?"

"Yes, it was approved," she replied. "You have a zero balance."

All I could do was give God the praise! I asked the clerk if she could send me a copy of the approval letter. After receiving and opening the letter, I saw to my amazement that a Non-Profit Organization had paid the bill!

My point in sharing this testimony with you is for you to grasp and comprehend that God wants to favor YOU! Are you humble enough to receive His favor? I was in a vulnerable place, but I received divine favor! I was in a place where I needed help and I had to humble myself to receive that help. I was not going to allow the spirit of Pride to withhold my blessing. I am now free of the $94,000 debt! Thank God that favor is my Kingdom Portion! And... Favor is Your Kingdom Portion!

Chapter 8: Favor is Your Kingdom Portion
Application for My Life

1. What is a popular cliché in many Christian circles?

2. Who came to Mary to deliver a message?

3. What was that message?

4. Name a scripture that talks about the favor of God.

5. What scriptural passage reveals to us that Hannah had more children?

6. How many sons did Hannah have?

7. Can you work or pay for the favor of God?

Answers to Life Application Questions

1.

2.

3.

4.

5.

6.

7.

WHERE WILL YOU SPEND ETERNITY?

This is the most important question that you will ever encounter. Mankind has always questioned life after death. Consequently, people live their lives as if they are not concerned about where they will spend eternity. According to Hebrews 9:27 everyone has an appointment with death. This is one appointment that you cannot reschedule or cancel. The following points will give you insight on why you need salvation and where you will spend eternity if accepted or rejected.

- **Sin separates us from God** – (Romans 3:23) Because of Adam and Eve's rebellion, we were all born with a nature bent away from the Lord.

- **Jesus was sent to make the payment for sin** – (1 Corinthians 15:3). Only the death of one who was perfect would satisfy the Father's righteous judgment. Jesus lived a life without sin, which qualified Him to become our substitute. He willingly took our place and died on the cross to pay our penalty. God accepted His death in place of ours and declared us righteous in His sight (Rom. 3:22).

- **Salvation is a free gift, received through faith in Jesus** (Eph. 2:8-9). Our good works will neither satisfy divine justice nor pay for our transgressions. They are not what God requires for forgiveness or adoption into His family. Faith in Jesus is the only way to God (John 14:6). When we accept Christ as our Savior and Lord, heaven becomes our eternal destination.

- Is your name written in the Lamb's Book of Life?– This book records the name of every person that accepted Jesus gift of salvation. (Revelation 21:27) If you reject the gift of salvation your name will not appear in this book. Every unbeliever that die in that state will go to a temporary place of torment call Hades or Hell. They will be judged at the Great White Throne Judgement (Revelation 20:11), and the lake of fire is their eternal destination.

<u>Prayer for Salvation</u>

Jesus, I want to be a part of your family. I acknowledge my sins and repent of them and receive your forgiveness. I believe that You came and died for me and was raised from the dead, and I accept YOU as my Lord and Savior. I receive your Holy Spirit to transform me into your image daily as I study your word. I am now saved. Jesus is my Lord. Jesus is my Savior. Thank you, Father God, for forgiving me, saving me, and giving me eternal life with You. Amen!

JESUS DON'T LEAVE EARTH WITHOUT HIM!

About the Author

Connie Strickland is an apostolic voice for this age and a marketplace leader in the Kingdom. She is the overseer of CSMI, Connie Strickland Ministries International, where she travels globally preaching the kingdom message; and a General of Intercession at AHOP (Apostolic House of Prayer) where she is equipping, training, and empowering intercessors to cover the Earth with prayer through the 8 prayer watches. She has served in ministry for over 30 years.

Apostle Connie Strickland has a passion to help others fulfill their destiny and purpose in life and have often been called the *"midwife apostle"*. She empowers many through her books and teachings on social media platforms. Apostle Connie is the President and CEO of Destiny Publishing Group LLC, Integrity Tax Services LLC, and Rainbow Productions. She is also a professional writing coach, ghostwriter, publisher, and author. Apostle Connie's desire is to complete her assignment in the Earth and simultaneously enjoy life with her family and friends. She is the mother of 3 adult children and 3 grandchildren. Please visit her social media platforms to get more information or to request her for kingdom assignments.

Purchase books @ PayPal.Me/destinypublishing

Lord Teach Me How to Pray
The Secret Place
A Celebration of Celibacy in a Sex Driven World *(For Single Adults)*

New Releases – August 2020

Kingdom Identity – Volume 1
The Revealed God
The Blessing of Afflictions

Fiction – Fall of 2020

The Blind Man

Contact Information
Email: cmstrick43@gmail.com
Facebook, Instagram

Made in United States
North Haven, CT
19 September 2022

24315465R00061